BEGINNERS GUIDE TO
WINDOWS 10

Lynn Stephen

CONTENTS

Chapter Twelve

INTRODUCTION

Windows 10 is Microsoft's latest operating system and hopefully will be around for quite a while. It is much easier to use than the previous system, Windows 8, which many people found very confusing with all the various tiles on the home screen. Windows 10, however, is more like Windows 7 and is much friendlier and easier to use.

This book is written for new users to Windows 10 so if you have just upgraded from Windows 7, 8 or 8.1 to Windows 10 then hopefully you will find this book useful.

Similarly, if you are completely new to computers then the opening chapters of the book are primarily aimed at you and cover the basics of computing i.e. your computer, monitor, keyboard and mouse.

If you are new to computers or just new to Windows 10, I hope this book will soon have you using your computer with great confidence.

CHAPTER ONE

YOUR COMPUTER

When you buy a new computer it will usually consist of four main components, the computer, the monitor (screen), the keyboard and the mouse. If you opt for a laptop, all the components are together. You may also have a printer.

Before I go into detail regarding these items, I would like to explain a few words you may come across and which may cause some confusion regarding your computer:

HARDWARE - the main components of your computer (tower, monitor, keyboard, mouse, and printer) are known as hardware. Hardware refers to components which you can see. All of these components work together and are connected via cables, or wirelessly, to your computer.

SOFTWARE - to enable a computer to function it must use software. Software is a program which is either pre-installed onto your computer or which comes on a

CD/DVD. The CD or DVD would be inserted into the CD drive on your computer, which would enable the relevant program to be installed onto your computer. Once the software has been installed, it will stay on your computer's hard drive. The CD will be removed and kept in a safe place. A good example of software is your word processing program, Microsoft Word.

OPERATING SYSTEM - Windows 10 is your operating system. This is the most important piece of software on your computer. Without it your computer will not work. It is called "Windows" because every time you open a new file or program, it will open in a new window. The window can be made to fill the whole screen or can be minimized or restored down to one third of its size.

HARD DRIVE (C: Drive) - this is the main storage in your computer and is located inside your computer or laptop so it is not actually visible.

CD/DVD DRIVE - this refers to a drawer on the front of your computer or on the side of your laptop, into which you insert CDs or DVDs to either install a program or to listen to music or watch a film.

USB – Many computers will have one or more USB ports. USB stands for Universal Serial Bus. These ports enable you to connect a device such as a printer or camera to your computer.

APPS – Applications. There are many apps which you can download onto your computer from the Windows Store. There are office based apps, reference apps, games and many more, all of which can be found at the Windows Store for which there is an icon on your task bar

Types of Computer

Two examples of computer.

Tower and a more compact computer.

Computers come in all shapes and sizes, you can have a tower or a smaller more compact computer which can sit on your desk.

Many people believe it is the monitor, which is the computer, which is an easy mistake to make, as it is the monitor you are looking at when you are using the computer.

It is on the front of the computer that the power button is located. This is the button which will turn your computer on (known as booting up). There may also be a smaller button on the front of the computer, which is the reset button. This will enable you to restart your computer without completely turning it off (known as rebooting). You may need to use this button should everything on your computer freeze but don't worry too much as this doesn't happen much these days.

Also on the front of your computer there will be a disc drawer with a small button next to it which, when pressed will open the drawer and it is here that you will place a CD or DVD.

CHAPTER TWO

THE MONITOR

The monitor or screen is where you will see all the images on your computer and all the text, which you type in. When you first switch on your computer you will see a small arrow in the centre of the screen, this is called the cursor. The cursor is positioned on objects on the screen using your mouse. You will then click on the object and the program will open.

CHAPTER THREE

THE KEYBOARD

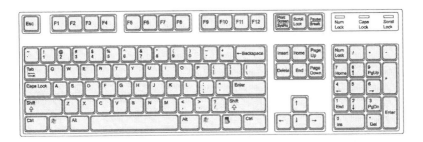

The keyboard is used to type text, which will appear on the screen. The main keys on a keyboard are arranged in the same way as on a typewriter. There are two main types of keyboard, a wired keyboard i.e. one, which is connected to your computer via a cable, and the other is a wireless keyboard, which has a USB dongle, which is plugged into your computer. The wireless keyboard will pick up the signal from the dongle in your computer. This will then enable you to use your keyboard without being restricted by a wire.

I will now explain the keys on your keyboard. There are many different types of keyboard, which may be laid out in different ways with shortcut keys, but generally, the main keys are the same.

ESC key. This is the escape key and can be used in various situations. Some programs will tell you to press the escape key to get out of the program. People who play games on their computers often use this key to exit the game. Another example of its use is on the Internet when you have a program such as BBC iPlayer playing on full screen, you would need to press this key to return to a normal size screen.

F KEYS. Along the top of your keyboard, you will see a row of keys from F1 to F12. These keys are called Function keys and generally, they are not used when you are beginning. The exception being the F1 key, which will bring up a help menu in any program and the F4 key which, when pressed with the Alt key, will close the current window. As a beginner, you can ignore these keys.

PRINT SCREEN, SCROLL LOCK AND PAUSE BREAK KEYS. These are located next to the function keys. The Print Screen key enables you to take a screenshot of the image you are viewing and save it or send it by email. The Scroll Lock key is used mainly in Excel, which is a spreadsheet program, and it enables you to move the window without moving the selected cell. The Pause Break key, when pressed with the Windows logo key, will bring up information about your computer.

TAB key. On many word processing programs, there are pre-set tabs on the page and each time you press the tab key you will move to the next tab point on the page. You can also set your own tabs on a page. When filling out forms on the Internet i.e. when registering on a website, you are asked to fill in several boxes; name, address, email address etc. By pressing the tab key, you can quickly move to the next box without having to use your mouse.

CAPS LOCK key. When this key is pressed once, everything you type will be in capital letters. Remember to press it again to return to normal typing.

SHIFT key. The shift key is used to type one capital letter. Hold this key down while you press the required letter. As soon as it is released, you will return to normal type. You have two Shift keys, one at each end of the keyboard. You will notice on your keyboard several keys with multiple characters. By holding down the shift key and pressing the relevant key, you will type the character at the top of this key (by pressing number 1 you will type the exclamation mark, which is at the top of this key).

CTRL key. This is the Control key which when pressed with other keys will enable you to take various shortcuts depending on which program you are in at the time. Pressing CTRL and S will save your work, CTRL and P will print your work.

WINDOWS LOGO key. This key when pressed will bring up the start screen. In addition, when you are in a program, pressing this key will return you to the start screen. In Windows 10, you will probably use this key at lot.

ALT key. This key is used for various shortcuts. i.e. Alt and F4 will close the window currently open.

THE SPACEBAR. This is the long bar at the bottom of your keyboard and is used to put a space between words.

THE FOUR DIRECTIONAL ARROW KEYS. The up and down arrows will enable you to scroll the page up and down. When in a word processing program all four directional arrows can be used to move around the page.

ENTER key. This key is used to give a command to your computer. If you are searching for something on the Internet, after you have typed a subject into the search box, by pressing the Enter key this will send the information and give you the results. In a word processing program, pressing the enter key will take you to the next line.

BACKSPACE and DELETE keys. These keys are used to delete typed text. By pressing the backspace key once, you will delete the last letter typed to the left of the cursor. By pressing the delete key once, you will delete the last letter typed to the right of the cursor. If you hold either of these keys down it will continue to delete until the relevant key is released. The backspace key can also be used on the Internet to go back to the previous page.

INSERT key. This key is used in word processing to overtype everything to the right of the cursor. Normally this key is not activated so if you wish to use it you need to turn it on. To do this right click on the status bar at the bottom of the screen (status bar is the bar at the bottom of the word processing page) and then click on overtype. You will then see the word Insert on the left of the status bar. If you now press the Insert key this word will change to Overtype. Whatever you now type will replace the words already there. Don't forget to press it again to revert to normal typing.

HOME and END keys. These keys can be used in conjunction with the CTRL key. For example, if you press CTRL and Home you will immediately be taken to the top of the page. Similarly, if you press CTRL and End you will be taken to the bottom of the page.

PAGE UP and PAGE DOWN keys. These keys do exactly as they say. By pressing page up the page will move up and by pressing page down, the page will move down.

NUM LOCK key. This key has two uses. If you press this key so the function is on, you can type the numbers from the small panel on the right of the keyboard. If you press it again and take the function off, the keys on this small panel can be used to scroll around your page.

NUM LOCK, CAP LOCK, SCROLL LOCK indicator lights on the keyboard inform you if any of these functions are on. If the light is on, the function is on. For example if the Cap Lock light is on, this is an indicator that you have chosen to type in capital letters. I find this is a very useful reminder, as it is very easy to forget to turn the cap lock off.

CTRL, ALT and DELETE. By holding these keys down all at the same time, you can end a non-responsive program. Pressing the keys will take you to a screen where you should click on task manager where you will then see all running programs. Just click on the non-responsive program in the list, and then click on "end task" at the bottom.

CHAPTER FOUR

THE MOUSE

The mouse is a device, which you use to point to things on the screen. When you move the mouse, you will see a small arrow (cursor) on the computer screen. You use the cursor to select the desired program or object. The cursor must be on the program or object concerned. You will then be required to click, either once or twice, on the program to open it.

There are two types of mice; a wired mouse, which is connected to your computer via a cable, or a wireless mouse, which has a USB dongle, which is connected to your computer. The wireless mouse then picks up the signal from the dongle in your computer and you are not restricted by a wire.

The mouse has several different functions. Before we can begin, you need to know how to use your mouse.

It is a good idea to place your hand over the mouse so you feel comfortable and relaxed and so that your index finger on your right hand (assuming you are right handed) is resting over the left hand button of the mouse. Ideally, with your hand relaxed you can now move your mouse to position the cursor on the required program or object and then click on the object without taking your eyes off the screen.

Do not worry if you are having difficulty in controlling your mouse, everyone has trouble at first - just try to relax your hand.

Mouse Functions

Left Click - this means you should use the left side of your mouse to click once on the specified object or program. This is the most frequently used function of the mouse and is used to give the computer an instruction. Although a double left click is often used to get into a program, it is nearly always a single left click when you are in the actual program.

Double Click - this instruction is used to open a program, folder, file etc. You should click on the left side of the mouse twice in quick succession.

Right click - by clicking on an object using the right side of the mouse, you will be presented with a menu specific to the item you have just clicked on.

Scroll - almost every mouse will have a scroll wheel in the centre. You can move this wheel forward and back which in turn will move your page up and down. Just gently roll the wheel either up or down. Do not press too hard on this scroll wheel otherwise the page will scroll out of control. If this does happen, press the wheel again and it should return to normal.

Drag - this involves placing your cursor on an item, holding down the left side of the mouse and keeping it held down, dragging the item to the desired position. This function can be used on the Start screen to rearrange the tiles displayed here. This is also useful when placing files into folders.

CHAPTER FIVE

PRINTERS

There are many different Printers and it would be impossible for me to go into detail on any of these, as the printer you buy would probably be different.

However most people nowadays will opt for an "All in One Printer". This is a printer, scanner and photocopier all in one machine. These are very popular and very useful.

Most are stand-alone photocopiers so you do not need to switch your computer on to take a photocopy.

You can scan documents or photos from your all-in-one printer to your computer and view them on the screen.

If you are using a laptop then it is a good idea to buy a wireless printer, in which case the printer could be in one room and you can print from another room. This is ideal if you do not have much room.

You can also use a wireless printer with a desktop computer but if you have room and can place the printer near your computer then I think to have it connected by a wire is a better way to go.

CHAPTER SIX

LAPTOPS

If you have chosen a laptop then everything already written is relevant to you but I will cover the basic differences between a laptop and a desktop computer.

With a laptop, instead of having four different components to make your computer work, everything is contained within one machine.

When you open your laptop, you will see the keyboard at the bottom and the screen at the top. The power button on your laptop will be positioned somewhere just above the keys on the keyboard. Press this once and your laptop will power on.

On the keyboard just below the spacebar, you will see a small rectangle pad. This is called your touchpad and it is this pad, which you will use to control your cursor,  in the same way you would use a mouse on a desktop computer. You move your finger gently over this pad and you will see the cursor on the screen move. You can now position the cursor on an item. Just below the touchpad, there are two buttons and these correspond to the left and right buttons on a mouse. Pressing the left button corresponds to a left click on a mouse. On the touchpad, be careful not to go too close to the right and bottom sides of the pad when you are first starting out as these have scroll functions on. If you accidentally move your finger up and down on the right side, you will notice the page zoom up or down. Just move away from the right side of the touchpad and it will return to normal.

These scroll functions on the touchpad can be used to scroll the page up and down in addition to the up and down directional arrow keys on the keyboard.

If you have trouble mastering the touchpad, and many people do, you can always use a wireless mouse instead. You would plug in the USB dongle, which comes with a wireless mouse into the relevant slot on your laptop, and the mouse will pick up the signal. You can now use the mouse as you would with a desktop computer.

On the side of your laptop, you will have a CD/DVD drive drawer and in the centre of this drawer, you will see a small raised button. Press this once and the drawer will pop out. Place a CD/DVD in the drawer and push the drawer back in to play the disc.

Charging your Laptop

Your laptop will have come with a battery and a charger/power lead. It is important not to overcharge your laptop, as this will dramatically reduce the life of your machine. Ideally, you should plug your laptop in and use on mains power until the battery is fully charged. Once fully charged, you should unplug your laptop and use on battery power. Once the battery gets low, a message will appear on the screen asking you to switch to mains power. This is the time to again plug your laptop in.

You can easily see the status of your battery by moving your cursor to the bottom right of the screen and positioning it over the battery symbol (no need to click). It will now show you the battery percentage and how much time you have left before you need to charge it again.

CHAPTER SEVEN

ANTI-VIRUS SOFTWARE

It is very important for you to have up-to-date anti-virus software installed on your computer to eliminate the possibility of your computer being infected with a virus.

If you are unfortunate enough to be infected with a virus, your computer will become unresponsive and you will need to seek help from a computer engineer to remove the virus. This may involve you losing all your files and programs as your hard drive may have been infected and will need to be formatted and Windows reinstalled.

There are many expensive anti-virus programs on the market but these are not necessary.

Windows 10 comes with its own antivirus program installed. This is called Windows Defender. To quickly find this program, type in the Cortana box on your Task Bar "Windows Defender" and it should be at the top of the list as the best match, see following. Click on this.

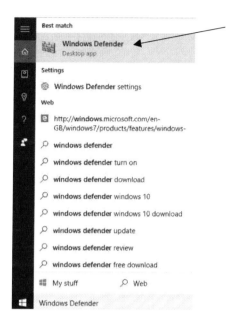

Windows Defender will now appear on the screen. See following.

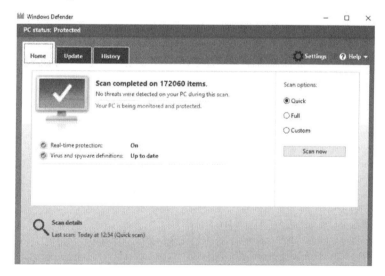

If you see a green bar at the top of the page (see previous pic) then your computer is protected.

Many people are under the impression that if they have an anti-virus program installed on their computer they are protected. This is not the case, as you must regularly scan your computer for viruses.

Completing a Scan of your Computer

In order to keep your computer protected you will need to carry out regular scans. To do this you should open Windows Defender and on the right of the page you should click in the circle to the left of Full (i) and then click on Scan Now (ii). See following.

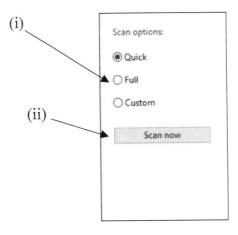

I would recommend that you carry out a full scan once a month and a quick scan once a week.

Obviously you cannot be 100% sure you will never get a virus but having anti-virus software installed reduces this risk dramatically.

Putting Windows Defender on the Task Bar

So that you can easily find Windows Defender, you should place it on the task bar at the bottom of your Start screen. To do this, when Windows Defender is open you will see a brick wall (symbol for Windows Defender) on the Task Bar, right click on this and then click on "Pin to Taskbar". This will now permanently be on the taskbar and you can open it quickly and easily from here.

CHAPTER EIGHT

GETTING STARTED WITH WINDOWS 10

Start Screen

The first screen you see when you switch on your computer will be very similar to the following:

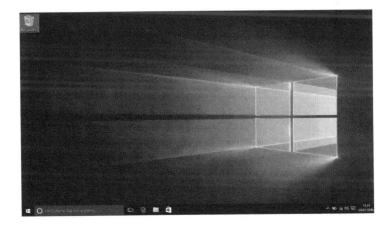

This is your start screen. At the bottom of this screen is a bar called the Task Bar and on this bar are various small icons which I will explain on the following pages.

Task Bar

Below is a picture of the left side of the Task Bar.

Start Button
(Windows Key)

File Explorer

Task View

Cortana

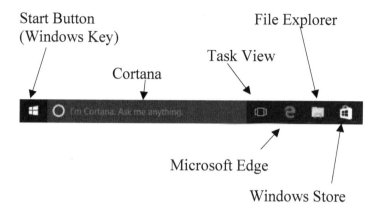

Microsoft Edge

Windows Store

Start Button

When you click on the Start Button (or press the windows key on your keyboard) you will see the start Menu.

On the left of the start menu are the most used applications (apps) and on the right are tiles, some of which are live tiles, which update all the time. You can move tiles, delete tiles or add tiles to this screen.

Below is a picture of the start menu.

The tiles on the right of this screen represent programs which are most likely to be used such as Microsoft Edge, Email, People and Photos.

You can add tiles to this menu as well as moving, resizing or deleting tiles from here.

Adding apps to the Start Menu

You can easily add tiles to the start menu by first clicking on All apps at the bottom left hand side of the start menu. See following.

You will see on the left hand side a list in alphabetical order of all the apps, which are installed, on your computer. See following.

Scroll Bar

On the right of this menu is a scroll bar, which will move the list up and down. Find the app, which you would like to move to the start menu, right click on it and then click on "Pin to Start" (see following picture). Your app will now appear below the tiles to the right of the menu.

Moving Tiles around on the Start Menu

When you have your tiles on the Start Menu, you may wish to move them around, i.e. having the most used tiles at the top. To move a tile, click on it and holding down the left side of the mouse or touchpad, drag the tile to the required position on the Start Menu.

Deleting tiles from the Start Menu

In order to delete tiles from the start menu, you should right click on the app you wish to delete and then click on Unpin from Start. This does not delete the program from your computer, just the tile from your start menu.

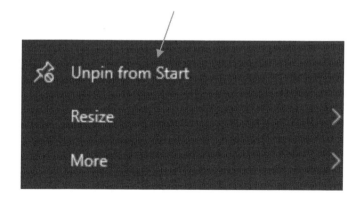

Resizing Tiles on the Start Menu

To resize tiles on the Start Menu, you should right click on a tile and then click on Resize when a further menu will appear - see following.

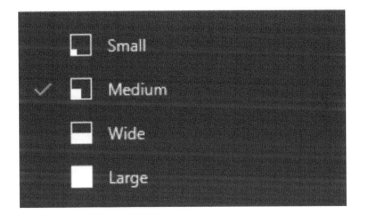

You should now click on the option required and the tile will resize accordingly.

Cortana

You will see on your Taskbar a box next to the start button showing "Ask me anything" see following.

Simply click in the box and type in a question or click on the microphone symbol and speak to your computer (you will need a microphone on your computer for this part of Cortana to work).

You can ask Cortana to remind you of an appointment or remind you to make an important phone call.

You can also type in the name of a file, folder or program on your computer and it will be located for you.

Task View

If you have several programs open, you can quickly switch between them by clicking on this icon. You will then see all open programs, see following.

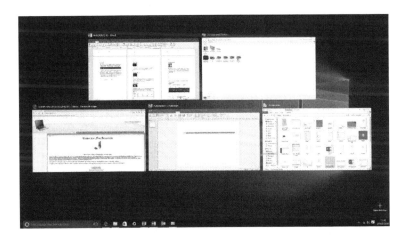

Simply click on the program you wish to work on.

Microsoft Edge

Microsoft Edge is the new browser for Windows 10 and replaces Internet Explorer. This is the program you will use to access the internet. *See Chapter 12.*

File Explorer

By clicking on this icon you can quickly access your documents and pictures folders – see following.

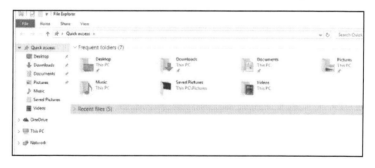

Windows Store

By clicking on this, you will be taken to the Windows Store where you are able to download apps to your computer.

Although there are many apps already installed on your computer, there are hundreds more in the Windows Store.

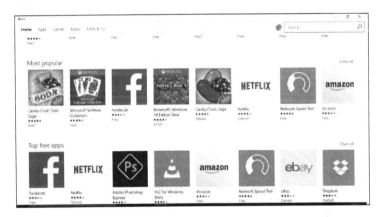

Most of the everyday apps are free. To download an app, click on the app required, you should then click on "free" and the app will start to download. Once downloaded you will find the app in your start menu either under "recently added" or under "all apps". Click on the app to open.

You can of course move your new app to the start menu by following the instructions on pages 30/31.

Below is a picture of the right side of the Task Bar

Show Hidden
Icons

Sound

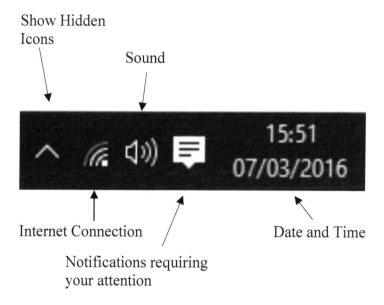

Internet Connection

Notifications requiring
your attention

Date and Time

Show Hidden Icons

There are a few icons which are hidden from view on
the taskbar. By clicking on this symbol you will see the
hidden icons.

Internet Connection

This shows that you are connected to the internet. If at
any time, there is a red exclamation mark on this
symbol you may have a problem with your internet
connection.

Sound

By clicking on this symbol, you will be able to increase or decrease the volume on your computer.

Notifications

This is where any notifications, you need to be made aware of, are shown. For instance, if you have not run your antivirus program for some time, it will notify you that this needs to be done.

Date and Time

This is the current date and time. You should click on this should you wish to make changes to the date or time. You should then click on "Date and Time

Settings" at the bottom of this window and you will be able to change the date or time.

Recycle Bin

Also on the start screen is the recycle bin. If you delete anything from your computer, be it a document or picture or maybe some music, it will be placed in the Recycle Bin. It will stay in the Recycle Bin until you empty the bin when it will be gone for good.

To empty the bin, you should right click on the Recycle Bin icon and you will see the following menu.

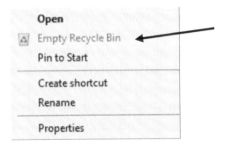

Click on Empty Recycle Bin and you will be asked if you are sure you wish to delete the items in the bin – see following.

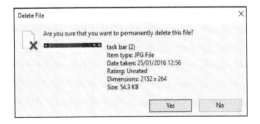

Click on yes and the items will be removed.

CHAPTER NINE

TURNING OFF YOUR COMPUTER

To turn off your computer you should first click on the Start Button or press the windows key on your keyboard. You should then click on Power (see below).

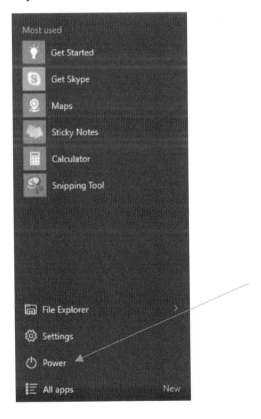

You will then see a small menu appear and you should now click on Shut Down, see following.

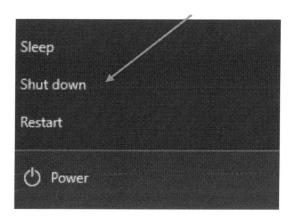

Your computer will now be turned off. Sometimes when you turn your computer off, you will see a message on the screen stating that updates are being installed – this is perfectly normal and you do not have to do anything. The computer will turn itself off when the updates have been installed.

CHAPTER TEN

PEOPLE

This app is your address book where all your contacts will be stored. To access this app, you should first click on the start button and then click on all apps, at the bottom. You will find the people app in this list.

Click on People in this list and the app will open. See following.

Adding a New Contact

In order to add a contact to your address book, you should click on the + symbol at the top of this window. You will then see a window similar to the following.

NEW OUTLOOK CONTACT

Add
photo

Name

Mobile phone ∨

+ Phone

Personal email ∨

+ Email

+ Address

+ Other

From here, you should fill in the relevant boxes on this page. You need only fill out the boxes you require i.e. just name and email is fine.

Click in the relevant box; wait for the flashing cursor to appear, and then type in the information. When you have finished filling in the required information you should click on the symbol at the top right of the page – see following.

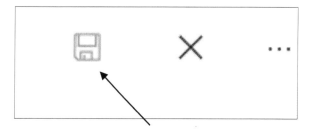

Your contact will then be saved into your address book. To add another contact, follow the above steps by first clicking on the + symbol at the top left of the page.

Editing a Contact

Should one of your contacts change their email address then you would need to edit their details. To do this you should first click on the contact to edit and then click on the pen symbol at the top right – see following.

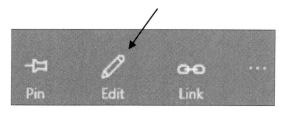

You can now amend the details you have for this contact. When you have done this remember to click on the save symbol at the top of the page otherwise your changes will not be saved.

<u>Deleting a Contact</u>

In order to delete a contact from your address book, you should first click on the unwanted contact. You should then click on the three dots at the top right of the window – see following.

You should now click on Delete on the small menu, which has now appeared.

You will then see a further window asking if you wish to delete this contact – click on Delete and your contact will be deleted.

By adding Contacts to your address book, it will make sending emails to your contacts much easier - see following chapter on emails.

CHAPTER ELEVEN

EMAIL

Setting up your Email

To set up your emails, you should first click on the start button and then click on the Mail tile on the right side of the start menu – see above icon.

When you have clicked on this, you will see the following appear.

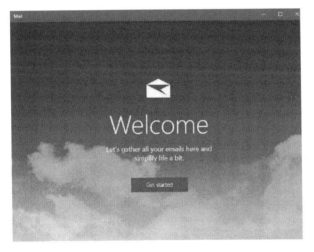

Click on Get Started in the centre of the screen and you will see the following screen.

Click on Add Account in the centre and you will then see the following.

Adding a Microsoft Account

If you want to set up the email address you use with your Microsoft account, you should click on the top option i.e. Outlook.com, Live.com, Hotmail, MSN. You will then see a window similar to the following.

Enter your email address and password in the relevant boxes and then click on Sign in at the bottom of the window and you will then see the following confirmation that your account has been set up.

Click on Done at the bottom and you will be taken to your email account where any new emails will be shown.

Adding a Gmail Account

If you have a Gmail email address, then you should click on Google on the list as shown on page 52, and the following window will appear.

You should now enter your Gmail email address in the box in the centre of the page and then click on Next where you will be asked to enter your password. You should now click on sign in. On the next window you should click on Allow at the bottom – see following.

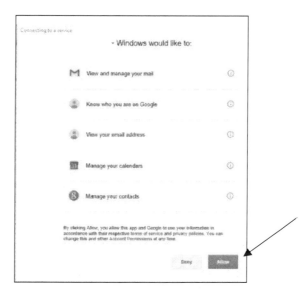

You will then see the following window. Type your name into the box at the top.

When you have typed in your name, you should click on "Sign in" at the bottom of the window.

You will then see a window confirming that your account has been successfully set up.

Click on done at the bottom and you will be taken to your email account where any new emails will be shown.

Setting up a another email Account i.e. btinternet, talktalk, sky, etc

If you have one of these email addresses, then you should choose Other account from the following list.

You will then see the following window appear.

Other account

Email address

someone@example.com

Password

We'll save this information, so you don't have to sign in every time.

Cancel   Sign-in

Enter your email address and password in the relevant boxes and then click on "Sign in" at the bottom. You will then see the following confirming that your email has been set up.

Click on Done at the bottom and you will be taken to your email account where any new emails will be shown.

Reading Emails

When you open the Mail app, you will be taken straight into your Inbox and any new messages will be shown here. See following. You will see this window is split into three sections, the first of which displays your email account and the various mailboxes i.e. Inbox, Sent Items. The second column is where any new messages will appear and the third column is where your messages will be displayed, whether you are reading a message or writing a new email.

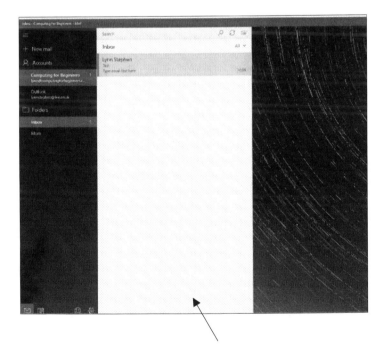

Any new emails will be shown in this column. To read the email you should click on it in this column and it

will open and be shown in the right hand column. See
following.

The message will be shown in full in this column.

Replying to an Email

If you wish to reply to an email you should click on Reply on the bar at the top of the page – see following.

You will then see a screen similar to the following. You will see the cursor flashing and you can just start to type. There is no need to insert an email address as this is automatically inserted when you click on reply.

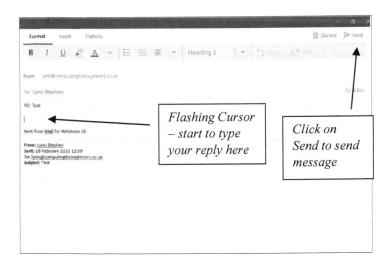

When you have typed your reply click on Send at the top right of the email window and your email will be sent and will be received within minutes.

Sending a new email message

To send a new message you should click on New Mail at the top of the first column – see following.

You will then see a window similar to the following.

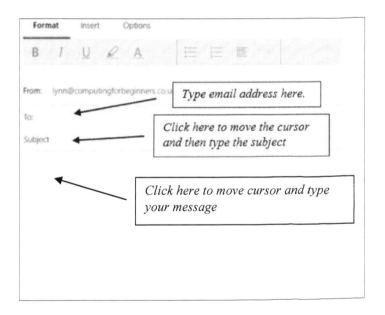

On this window, you will see a flashing cursor next to the word To: This is where you should type the email address of the person you are sending the message to (be very careful when typing the email address as a small mistake will result in the email not being sent).

If you have already added your Contacts to your address book in the People app, you only need to type the first initial of the person you are sending the message to. You will then see the email address appear, click on this to insert it.

You should then click next to the word Subject until you see the flashing cursor move to this position. You should then type in a short subject. You should then click in the space under the subject line and when you see the flashing cursor, you should type your message.

When you have typed your message and are ready to send it, simply click on Send on the top right of the screen.

Forwarding an Email

Sometimes you receive an email, which you may wish to forward on to someone else. To do this you should click on forward at the top of the screen – see following.

You will then see a window similar to the following:

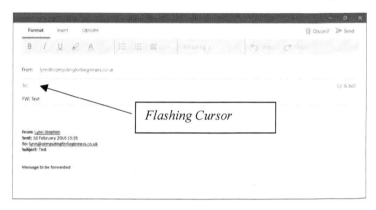

Flashing Cursor

The cursor will be flashing next to the word To: Type in here the email address of the person you wish to forward the message to. You should then click on send to send the message.

Deleting Emails

When you have read an email and you no longer wish to keep it, you should delete it. To do this you should click on Delete on the bar at the top of the page – see following.

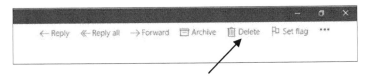

This will then place this message into your Deleted Items or Trash folder. It will not be permanently deleted until you clear your Deleted Items/Trash folder.

Clearing Deleted/Trash Folder

When you are sure that all the messages you have deleted are no longer required, you should empty this folder. To do this, you should click on the Deleted Items/Trash folder in your folder list and you will then see all the emails you have deleted – see following.

In order to delete all the emails at the same time, you should click on the first one and then hold down the Ctrl key on your keyboard and keeping it held down, press the A key. This will highlight all the emails and you can then click on delete at the top of the page. All the emails have now been permanently deleted.

Sending Attachments

In order to send an attachment with your email message, be it a document or a picture, you should click on Insert at the top of the email window – see following.

You should then click on Attach and your Documents folder will open.

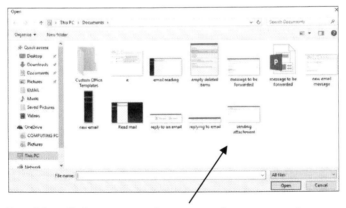

Double click on any document from your documents folder and it will be attached to your email.

Similarly if you are sending a picture with your email, you should click on Pictures in the menu on the left of the window – see following.

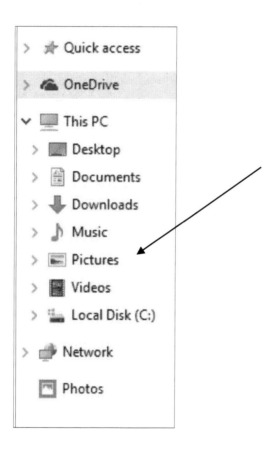

Your pictures will then be in view.

Double click on the picture you wish to send and it will be attached to your email.

Printing an Email

There are two ways to print an email. Firstly, you can hold down Ctrl on your keyboard and keeping this held down press the P button. Alternatively, you should click on the three dots at the top of the email window, and then click on print in the menu which then appears – see following.

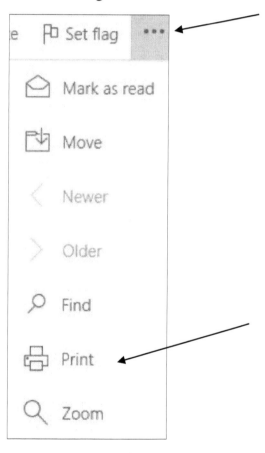

This will then bring up your printer window – see following.

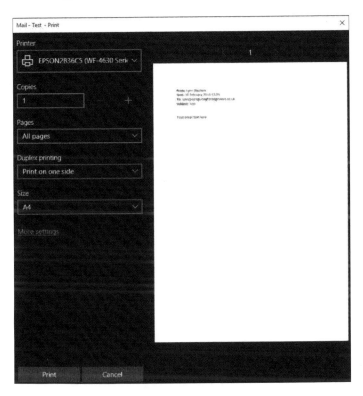

Your printer window will show a preview of the item to be printed on the right. On the left, you will see your printer name and at the bottom, you will see the word "Print". Click on this and the email will be printed.

Placing the Mail tile on your Taskbar.

When you have the Mail app open, you will notice an envelope symbol on the taskbar at the bottom of the screen. In order to add it to your taskbar, you should right click on it and then click on "pin to taskbar". Your mail icon is now on your taskbar and will remain there making it a quick and easy way to access your emails.

CHAPTER TWELVE

MICROSOFT EDGE

Microsoft Edge is the program you will use to explore the internet. This program is located on the task bar at the bottom of your screen. You can also access it from the start screen.

The internet is used to look things up, search for information, book holidays, online shopping, using social networking sites etc.

<u>Setting up Edge</u>

There are a few things you will need to do to set up Edge before you start to use it.

Your computer may have been set up with Google as your homepage but if not, I would recommend setting your homepage to Google as many people are familiar with this and it is very easy to use and is ideal for beginners to the internet.

The following steps will help you to set up Edge ready for use and will also set Google as your homepage.

1. Click on the three dots at the top right of the screen – see following.

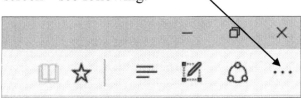

2. You will then see the following. Click on Settings.

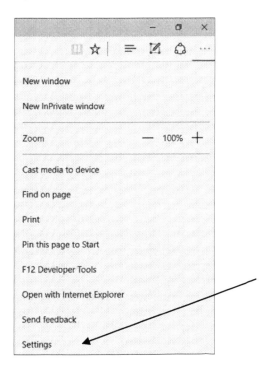

3. You will then see the following menu appear.
   Click on "A specific page or pages"

You should then click on the box which says
MSN and select Custom. See following.

Next click on the cross to delete the Microsoft website address – see following.

4. Click in the box "Enter a web address" and type in here www.google.co.uk – you should then click on the + symbol at the end of this box.

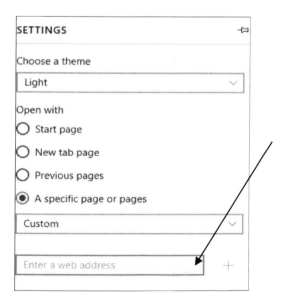

5. Further down the Settings menu click on "view favourites settings".

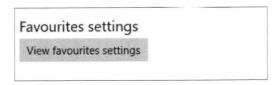

6. In the next menu which appears, you should click to the right of the black dot which will move it to the right and this will turn on your favourites bar.

You should then click on the « symbol next to the words Favourite settings to return to the Settings menu.

7. At the bottom of the Settings menu you should click on "view advanced settings"

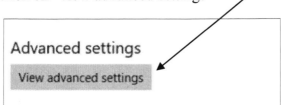

8. At the top of the Advanced Settings window, under the words "show the home button" you should click to the right of the black dot to turn this option on.

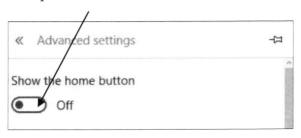

This will put a house symbol on your homepage which will enable you to return to your homepage from whatever page you are on.

9. In the box which has now appeared type in www.google.co.uk and then click on save underneath.

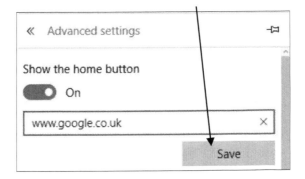

Click away from the settings menu to close it.

EDGE TOOLBAR EXPLAINED

Before you start to use the internet, I will explain all the symbols on the Edge toolbar at the top of the page. On the left of the bar, you will see the following symbols.

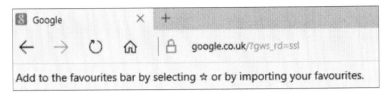

The first two symbols are your ***back and forward buttons.*** The left button will take you back a page and similarly the right button will take you forward a page.

This is your ***refresh*** button. If you are on a website and it is not responding, click on this symbol and it will refresh the page.

By clicking on this symbol, you will be returned to your *homepage.*

This is the *address bar* where you can type in a website address. The address bar will always show the address of the website you are viewing.

Add to the favourites bar by selecting ✰ or by importing your favourites.

This is your *favourites bar* and acts as a shortcut to your favourite websites.

On the right of the Edge bar, you will see the following symbols.

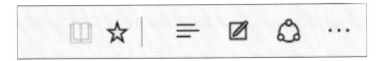

READING VIEW

 The first symbol is ***Reading View***. If this symbol is greyed out, then it is not available for the page you are viewing. If the symbol is black, you can click on it and it will turn blue and the website you are viewing will be shown without any ads and will be set out better for reading. The reading view in Edge is not available for many sites.

FAVOURITES

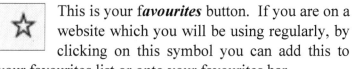 This is your *favourites* button. If you are on a website which you will be using regularly, by clicking on this symbol you can add this to your favourites list or onto your favourites bar.

When you click on this symbol you will see another menu appear – see following.

The second box on this menu asks you where you would like to save the website. If you would like to save it to a favourites list, then just click on Add at the bottom of the window. If you would like to save it to your favourites bar at the top of the page, click on the small downward arrow at the end of the second box and click on Favourites Bar (see following) and then click on Add at the bottom. This website will now appear on your favourites bar at the top of the screen.

Favourites bar

Any websites which are placed on your favourites bar can be easily accessed by simply clicking once on them. The website will then open.

READING LIST

When you click on the Favourites symbol, you will see a second item in the menu, which is *"Reading List"*. If you are on a particular website and wish to view it later, you can add it to your Reading List and it will then be available for you to view at another time.

Click on Add at the bottom to add website to your Reading List.

HUB CONTAINING FAVOURITES, HISTORY, READING LIST AND DOWNLOADS

When you click on this symbol, you are presented with four more symbols, which I will explain below.

Favourites list

By clicking on this symbol, you can access your favourites list. Any websites which you chose to add to your favourites will be shown here in a list format. Simply click on the website you wish to visit and it will open.

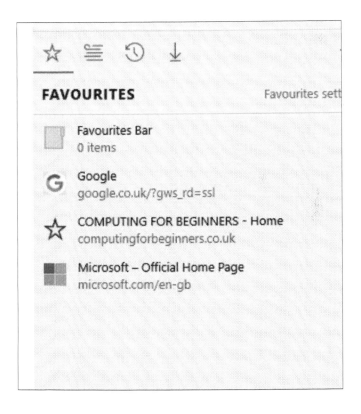

Reading List

By clicking on this symbol you will see all items placed in your reading list which you can access by simply clicking once on the required item.

History

By clicking on this symbol, you can view your browsing history. The history will be shown in date and time order. See following.

HISTORY	Clear all history
⊿ Last hour	✕
G Google google.co.uk/?gws_rd=ssl	15:17
↺ COMPUTING FOR BEGINNERS - Compute computingforbeginners.co.uk/page3.htm	15:17
↺ COMPUTING FOR BEGINNERS - Contact I computingforbeginners.co.uk/page6.htm	15:17
↺ COMPUTING FOR BEGINNERS - Home computingforbeginners.co.uk	15:15
▷ Earlier today – 22/2	✕
▷ Older	✕

Delete Browsing History

In order to delete your browsing history, you should click on "Clear all history" at the top of this menu. All traces of your browsing history will then be cleared.

Downloads

The final symbol on this menu is the Downloads symbol. When you click on this symbol, it will show all items which you have downloaded to your computer. You can clear this list by clicking on "clear all" at the top of this list.

WEB NOTES

The next symbol on the edge bar is the above, which represents web notes. You can draw and make notes on a website. You can then share these via email or social media i.e. twitter.

When you click on this symbol, you will notice that your tool bar will change to a purple colour and you will see the following symbols on the left of the tool bar.

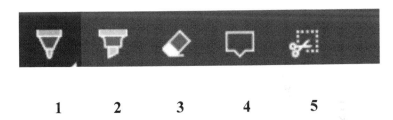

| 1 | 2 | 3 | 4 | 5 |

These symbols from left to right are:

1. ***Pen.*** Click on this symbol, *which* will enable you to draw or write notes on the webpage you are viewing. See following.

You will see I have drawn around the words Computing for Beginners.

2. *Highlighter pen.* Click on this symbol, *which* will enable you to highlight text on the page to bring attention to it. See following. You will see I have highlighted the words "One to One Computer Training in your own Home".

3. *Eraser.* If you make a mistake when you are writing a note, using the Pen or using the highlighter etc. just click on the eraser and move the cursor over the mistake and it will disappear.

4. *Add a Typed Note.* Click on this symbol and you will see that your cursor has changed to a ✛. Click where you wish to add a typed note and a box will appear into which you can type your note. See following.

If you make a mistake and wish to delete your typed note just click on the small dustbin in the bottom right of the box and your note will be deleted.

5. ***Clip.*** When you click on this symbol you will see the words "Drag to copy Region" in the centre of the screen – see following.

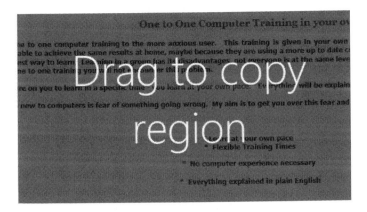

Place the cursor at the start of the text which you wish to copy, hold down the left side of the mouse and drag over the required text – see following:

* Learn at your own pace
* Flexible Training Times

* No computer experience necessary

* Everything explained in plain English

You will see that I have copied a section of text from my website.

When you have made your notes on the website and wish to either save or share this via email, you should look to the right of the toolbar where you will see the following symbols.

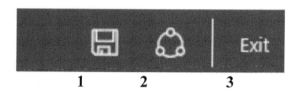

1. If you wish to save the notes you have made on the webpage to your favourites, you should click on the first symbol and you will see a menu appear similar to the following. Click on Add at the bottom to save.

2. If you wish to email a copy of the notes you have made on the website, you should click on the second symbol. You will then see a menu appear similar to the following.

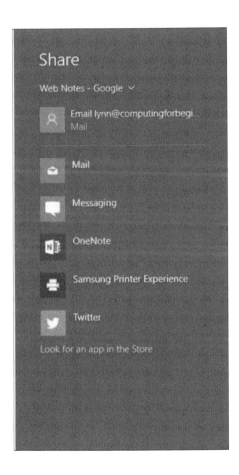

You should then choose the option required from this menu.

3. The final symbol on the bar is to exit the web note toolbar. Simply click on this and the webpage will return to normal.

SHARE

The next symbol on the edge bar is Share, which will enable you to share the webpage you are viewing via email or social media.

If you find a website, which you would like to share, click on this symbol and you will see a menu similar to the following.

Click on the option required from this menu, which will enable you to send a link to the webpage via either email or social media.

MORE SETTINGS

The final symbol on the edge bar gives you more settings.

This is the symbol you should click on to set your homepage, show the favourites bar and show the home button, all of which can be found at the beginning of this chapter.

<u>Printing from the Internet</u>

In order to print from the internet, you can either hold down the Ctrl button on your keyboard and then press P or click on the three dots, as shown above, and you will see a menu similar to the following.

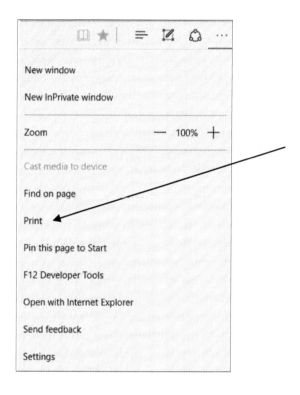

New window

New InPrivate window

Zoom   —   100%   +

Cast media to device

Find on page

Print

Pin this page to Start

F12 Developer Tools

Open with Internet Explorer

Send feedback

Settings

Click on Print and your printer window will appear.

CHAPTER THIRTEEN

HOW TO USE THE INTERNET

Now you have set up your homepage to Google, every time you click on Edge you will see a window similar to the following.

In the centre of the screen, immediately beneath the word Google, you will see a long box. See following.

You need to first click in this box until you see a flashing cursor, after which you should type in the subject you wish to search for.

Bear in mind that the more information you put in the search box, the better the results will be.

Once you have typed what you are looking for into the box, press enter on your keyboard and you will then see a long list of websites, which will be relevant to your search. You will see from the following image that I have searched for Computing for Beginners and a list of websites has appeared on the screen. My website is shown at the top.

You will always get a long list of websites relating to the subject you have searched for, sometimes thousands but I always find it is the first 15-20, which are most relevant.

To select one of the websites, you should click on the one you wish to look at (make sure the cursor is a hand before you click) and you will be taken to the website of your choice. I have clicked on my website and the next screen you will see is the homepage of your chosen website – see following.

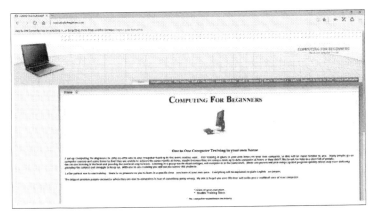

Every website will have a home page, which will show various links to different parts of that website. On my website, I have a few links at the top of the page, the first of which is Home.

To select one of these links, you should move your cursor, which at the moment is an arrow, over a heading and you will notice that the cursor has now changed to a hand allowing you to click and be taken to that part of the website.

If you then click on the Home link at the top of the website, you will be taken back to the homepage of the website. It is like turning the pages in a book to select a different chapter.

When you have finished looking at a website and wish to return to your homepage of Google, you should click on the house symbol on the toolbar at the top.

You can now do a fresh search following the above steps.

CHAPTER FOURTEEN

STAYING SAFE ON THE INTERNET

When and if you decide to buy things from the internet, there are two main things you must look out for. The first is a padlock symbol in the address bar at the top of the page. See following.

If you then click on the padlock symbol you will see a small window verifying the safety of the website and confirming that all information is encrypted – see following.

Furthermore if you click on the website address in the address bar i.e. amazon.co.uk you will see it change to https://amazon.co.uk – see following.

The "s" at the end of the "https" stands for secure. Please bear in mind you will only see the "https" when you click on the website address in the address bar and when you click back onto the website it will revert to the original with the padlock showing.

If you happen to go on to any website to make a purchase and are putting in personal information i.e. name, address and credit card details, and the padlock or the https are not present DO NOT continue as this website will not be secure.

Most well known websites will be safe but always check before entering any personal information.

CHAPTER FIFTEEN

ONEDRIVE

OneDrive is free online storage, which comes pre-installed on all Windows 10 computers.

By saving your documents and pictures onto OneDrive, you can easily access them from any other computer, tablet or phone by simply signing in to your Microsoft Account on that device.

One advantage of using online storage is that if your computer were to go wrong, your documents and pictures will be safe as they are backed up to OneDrive.

Saving Documents to OneDrive

If you have a Word document or similar which you wish to save to OneDrive, you should click on File at the top of the window – see following.

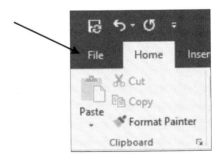

You should then click on Save As and you will see a window similar to the following.

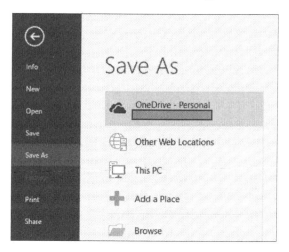

From here you should click on OneDrive – Personal. On the right of the page, type in a file name and then click on Save to the right. See following.

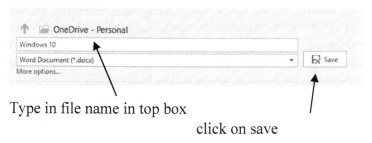

Type in file name in top box

click on save

Moving files to OneDrive

In order to move files from your computer to OneDrive you can simply drag them over from the File Explorer window.

You can see from the following picture that I am moving one of my pictures to OneDrive.

You should click and hold down the left side of the mouse on the picture or document, which you wish to move and then drag it over to OneDrive in the left-hand column.

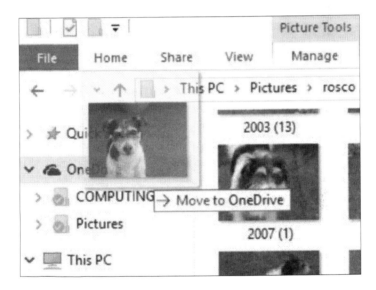

You will see that a small label will appear which states "Move to OneDrive". When this appears, just release the mouse and your photo or document will have been moved to OneDrive.

You can still access your files and pictures from your computer by clicking on File Explorer on the taskbar and selecting OneDrive from the left-hand column.

CHAPTER SIXTEEN

CHANGING YOUR DESKTOP BACKGROUND

When you get your new computer you may decide that you wish to change the background picture. You can either change this to another Microsoft desktop picture or you can have one of your own pictures as the background.

Changing to another Microsoft Background Picture

In order to do this, you should first right click anywhere in the centre of your start screen and this will bring up a menu – see following.

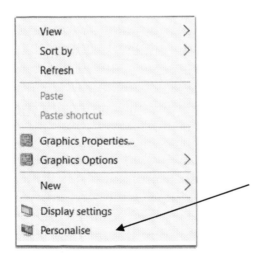

Click on Personalise and the following screen will appear.

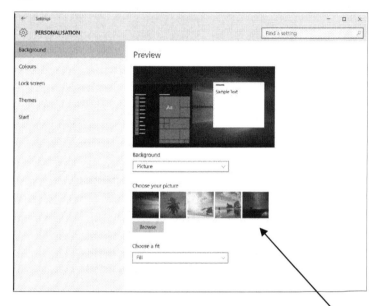

You can see the pictures available on this screen, underneath the words "Choose your picture". Click on the required picture and your desktop background would have been changed to your chosen picture.

Changing your Desktop Background to one of your own Pictures

To do this, you should first open up your pictures folder – see following.

You should then right click on the picture you wish to use when you will see a menu appear – see following.

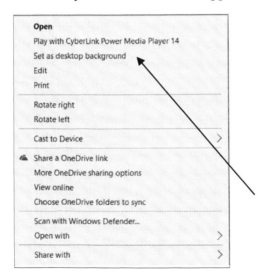

Click on "Set as desktop background" and your picture will be now showing on your desktop – see following.

ABOUT THE AUTHOR

Lynn Stephen recovered from a ten-year battle with ME in 1999 and re-trained in computers. She went on to obtain various City & Guild qualifications and in 2002, set up a computer training business "Computing for Beginners" which gives one to one computer and iPad training to the beginner.

For the past fourteen years, Lynn has been kept very busy with her training business and keeping up with all the latest changes in technology.

This is Lynn's sixth book, which she has been working on for the past few months, and which she hopes will help all of you who are new to Windows 10.

Lynn is married and lives in a small village in Kent with her Husband and her beloved Jack Russell, "Rosco".

Made in the USA
Charleston, SC
27 May 2016